*as I watch you*

*Grow*

*things I want you to*

*Know*

LETTERS TO MY DAUGHTER

*To my dear daughter*

*With all my love*

Made in the USA
San Bernardino, CA
12 November 2019

59761749R00058